THE GRE

THE GREGORY ANTHOLOGY 1991–1993

edited by
Dannie Abse and Anne Stevenson

SINCLAIR–STEVENSON

First published in Great Britain in 1994
by Sinclair–Stevenson
an imprint of Reed Consumer Books Ltd
Michelin House, 81 Fulham Road, London SW3
and Auckland, Melbourne, Singapore and Toronto

In this selection copyright © 1994 by The Gregory Trust
Introduction copyright © 1994 by Dannie Abse and Anne Stevenson
The copyright in individual poems remains with the poets

ISBN 1 85619 436 1

A CIP catalogue record for this book
is available at the British Library

Typeset by Deltatype Ltd, Ellesmere Port, Cheshire
Printed and bound in Great Britain by
Cox & Wyman Ltd, Reading

Contents

	Introduction	1
1991	WAYNE BURROWS	
	Biology Lessons	5
	The Flayed Elm	6
	The Dung-Beetle	7
	For a French Girl	8
	The Raft of Serpents	9
	JACKIE KAY	
	From The Adoption Papers	12
	RODDY LUMSDEN	
	Prayer to be with Mercurial Women	16
	The Bedroom at Arles	17
	Calendar	18
	Harpooneer	19
	Vanishing	20
	GLYN MAXWELL	
	La Brea	21
	Errand Boy	22
	Love Made Yeah	23
	Eyes and Bones on Song	24
	Out of the Rain, XXXVII	26
	STEPHEN SMITH	
	Letters to Myself, I–IV	27
	First Glance	30
	Ulster Holiday	31
	The Ringers	32
1992	JILL DAWSON	
	The Mechanic	35
	Arrina	37
	The Devil	38
	For My Sister	40
	Paean	41

HUGH DUNKERLEY
Swift Mockery   42
Geese   43
The Sea Skater   44
River   45

CHRISTOPHER GREENHALGH
Coffee-Break   46
Islands   47
From Here and Now   48
Stealing the Mona Lisa   49
The Night I Met Marilyn   50

MARITA MADDAH
Airborne   52
Our Brother   54
The Sunflowers   56
Song for Ali Tiko   58
Blood for Rain   60

STUART PATERSON
Sandend 1989   61
Gigha   62
Garrier at Midnight   63
Shroud   64
Silversmith   65

STUART PICKFORD
Over a Foreign Land   66
mother finally told the facts of her
   son's suicide   67
Cutting Dad's Nails   69
Port le Grand   70
Surrealism   72

1993 SEAN BOUSTEAD
To be Continued   77
Spring   78
Coming to Fields   79

Mid-Season	81
One-Way	82

ELEANOR BROWN
Pity	83
Bitcherel	85
Sonnets: II, III, VII, X, XI, XIV, XVI	86

TRACEY HERD
Artifice	90
Charades	91
A Terrible Day	92
The Cage	94
Marilyn Climbs Out of the Pool	95
A Searching Pace	96

JOEL LANE
The Silent Majority	97
Engaged	99
Energy and Silence	100
Messages	101
Gravel Tides	102

ANGELA McSEVENEY
Changing a Downie Cover	103
Blacking a Hearth Stone	104
Night Shift	105
Woman with Lilac Sash	106
My Crime	107
The Sweep	108

DERYN REES–JONES
The Ladies	109
The Chair	110
First	111
Following	112
I know exactly the sort of woman . . .	113

Biographical Notes	115
Acknowledgements	119

INTRODUCTION

This is the sixth anthology of poems by Gregory winners since the first awards were given in 1960 to young British poets by the then appointed judges, T.S. Eliot, Sir Herbert Read, Professor Bonamy Dobrée, Henry Moore and Howard Sergeant.

Dr E.C. Gregory, a successful publisher and printer, was all his life a generous patron of the arts. In the 1950s he established the Gregory Fellowships for poets and artists at the University of Leeds. After his death in 1959 the residue of the Gregory estate went to the Society of Authors, to be administered as a trust fund for the encouragement and financial assistance of promising poets under the age of thirty.

Every spring, a panel of seven judges meets to choose from a large number of applicants who have submitted book-length manuscripts. A short list is drawn up from which three to six young poets receive invitations for interview. Awards are primarily given for promise and ability.

The editors of the present anthology – both members of the current judging panel – have made a representative selection from the winning manuscripts over the past three years, 1991 to 1993. We believe that enough is included from the work of each poet to give a reader some idea of his or her individual voice and potential achievement.

No method of selection, of course, can ensure that over the years the judges have spotted every outstanding talent; but we do believe that this anthology is full of lively, independent-minded poems that signify a still-thriving art. Gregory winners in the past have included Geoffrey Hill, Michael Longley, Seamus Heaney, Douglas Dunn, Carol Ann Duffy and many other names well known in poetry today. It may be that, in the years to come, several of the young promising poets included here will be equally valued and renowned.

Dannie Abse and Anne Stevenson

1991

WAYNE BURROWS

Biology Lessons

'. . . no excellent beauty that hath not
some strangeness in the proportion.'

Francis Bacon

Here is the pathos of a stuffed monkey,
A jar of eyes from a child's bad dream,
A white rat flayed on a board with chrome
Pins, a thick, fruiting pungency on the air.
A child unlocks a skull, keeping count
Of each bone removed, while others admire
The cells of an inner-cheek, or endure
The dissection of a freshly-caught hare.

A girl wanders a line of shelves crammed
With bottles – *foetus*, *heart*, *larynx*, *tongue* –
Her eyes careful, her hand on the clock
Beating under her breast, and in her throat,
And the frail, rustling tug of her breath . . .
A recent hysterectomy contributes a cup
Of flesh, turning slowly in a womb of glass
That bears the inverted room like a lens.

Later, in a pure silence, sunlight streams
Through the still, green water of a tank
Where tadpoles turn from commas to frogs.
And here is a stirring near the Wormery –
Murky cortex, unwinding in a shaft of dust,
Its jar a sundial, a wand of rippling light
Cast between compassed initials, luminous
As an Aztec skull, a handful of fused quartz.

The Flayed Elm

The flayed elm keeps its vigil,
Wades in mist. The crescent moon,
Like a horned fruit hung low
In the hollow boughs, climbs slowly,
Counterweight to the drowned sun
On the sky's exact scales.

A cold wind lifts its hosts –
Paper, Straw, Leaves – takes the elm
As a mouth might a reed-pipe
(Or another mouth) to breathe a tide.
A fire drifts on its raft of bark,
A bright pollen of sparks, smoke,

The crackling and kettle-whine
At the heart of the blaze, high-
Pitched, almost a voice. And look!
An index-finger of flame stabbing
At stars sown in the cortex of cloud,
The moon at the top of the elm,

The dead wood crowned (stripped,
Desolate), the fire at its roots
Eerie in mist as a dropped halo
Stammering under rain. And now this,
An earth-lunged whispering from
The close-ribbed hills – *Come*.

The Dung-Beetle

(after Pennar Davies)

Simple, it gathers its shit in Spring
And rolls pellets of excrement to eat.
Selfless, too, sharing with feeble worms
And strong, white grubs the little it has,
Fattening creatures, loaming the soil,
Its tender loyalties perfected, its life
Honed to a strict, prophetic round
Of philanthropy and shit-shovelling.

What devotion, what humble prayers
At the altars of excrement stir
Its dull, primeval awarenesses?
Transcendence or alchemy, rolling buds
On the stalks of the early flowers,
Its great work a *Genesis* of shit
That reveals, forms a fragrant rose
From the rank filth of its purpose.

A close relative, and sacred in Egypt,
Scarabaeus was the World, confidant
To the Gods as it moved through dung
With its messages, its metallic shell
And violet legs scuttling on errands
In a patient Communion with shit.
Aristophanes praised it when it freed
Peace to assume her glorious reign,

And it could fly, but preferred to keep
To its own element, rolling, tunnelling . . .
Its lotus-flower antennae twitch,
Fumbling into light from dark manure,
And it might be deemed 'Insect of Gods'
Or the 'Saintly Beetle' that reveres
And revels in the lowest of spheres,
Serves the substance we most despise.

For a French Girl

(to Thérèse)

Half-squashed cornflake boxes
smell of sheep & goats, your
dog throws a trail of black &
ginger hairs on my lap.

You drive intently, the slightly
hooked nose pronounces a perfect
pidgin English, mine a pidgin
French. Scenery flashes in your
glasses, images of what the
watery blue eyes are thinking,

of farms & woodland, of cows
armoured in mud clattering
over the fields, the rubber
pipes pulling milk from fat
thick-veined udders.

You think on, admiring the roads,
your natural hair lopped off
at the shoulder. Newly mown hedgerows
scatter branches on our words.

The Raft of Serpents

(a wounded soldier, Nicaragua)

My right arm ends abruptly,
Severed at the elbow, laid out
On a bloodstained sheet
By my bruised, gangrenous side.
My left hand lacks fingers
With which to accuse, my thin
Voice rasps in its broken box.
Washington, I sigh. *Americans.*

In Florida, the dollars pile up
On account to the old regime,
While here, framed in the window
Over my bed, scorched fields
Blaze to a green forest's edge
And a few plump toddlers eat,
Scraping grey meal from a bowl
Outside their wrecked school.

Buses sway in under the weight
Of farmhands bored with war.
Their guns blink, their bodies
Shimmer in the haze and dust
As though not quite formed . . .

And try to imagine this scene –
The high sun casting leaf-shade
On the deep floors of a wood,
With three young men in green,
Barely accustomed to the feel
Of their boots, trampling twigs
And sprung loam – laughing.

We hadn't seen a soul all day,
Having set out in light mist
To watch the early sun forge
Its routine parabola. We ate well,
Our pockets full of wild fruit.
We chattered and smoked, laughed
Like crazy, convinced of privacy,
Until a single shell erupted
In a crack and spray of loam,
A cry and scattering of birds.

My hands were pulp, arms ribbons
Of bone and pulse. I cried out
As the smoke unveiled the dead,
Collapsed grins set in blood,
Fractured white plate, eyes . . .

I passed out. For a whole week
I lay there, almost dead. I felt
The cries of wild beasts prowl
Closer each half-conscious night,
Saw my friends' bones cleaned
By the slow grubbing of insects,
A pick of carrion birds' beaks.

Consciousness came then passed
While my memories churned out:
Children whose severed heads
And white limbs litter my past
Like those infernal dreams
I've fallen from, sweating cold
Under some lover's hands. I see
Their small ghosts stretching
Smoky fingers towards my face,

Lift my head, racked with pain
Like a wounded Christ, cut down,
Consigned to the round sun . . .
The great boughs form a Cross

Over my head, their haloed leaves
Sanctify me! My hate curls like
Burning books in my broken gut.

I am far from saintly. My hate
Extends its mad, black howling
To the furthest skirt of trees
At the edge of the wood. *Kill!*
I cried, and *Bastards!* and *Come!*
Like Quetzalcoatl, insane, starved,
I was a sack of bones and blood
So light that hunters bore me
Shoulder-high on a net of vines
Up ten miles of rough ground . . .

Now, I drift on my flayed back
In a heap of crumpled sheets,
Feel all the months of healing
Pass without change. Flayed God,
Cinteotl, I wait upon miracles.

Outside, under the blazing sun,
More small lives are consigned
(Bound in red felt) to the boot
Of a yellow bus. I, too, am dying.
I wear my mortal blows, dream up
Novel tortures for wicked men
And feed from a proffered spoon.

JACKIE KAY

From The Adoption Papers

4

I thought I'd hid everything
that there wasnie wan
give away sign Left

I put Marx Engels Lenin (no Trotsky)
in the airing cupboard – she'll no be
checking out the towels surely

All the copies of the Daily Worker
I shoved under the sofa
the dove of peace I took down from the loo

A poster of Paul Robeson
saying give him his passport
I took down from the kitchen

I left a bust of Burns
my detective stories
and the Complete Works of Shelley

She comes at 11.30 exactly.
I pour her coffee
from my new Hungarian set

And foolishly pray she willnae
ask its origins – honestly
this baby is going to my head

She crosses her legs on the sofa
I fancy I hear the Daily Workers
rustle underneath her

Well she says, you have an interesting home
She sees my eyebrows rise
It's different she qualifies

Hell and I've spent all morning
trying to look ordinary
– a lovely home for the baby

She buttons her coat all smiles
I'm thinking
I'm on the home run

But just as we get to the last post
her eye catches at the same time as mine
a red ribbon with twenty world peace badges

Clear as a hammer and sickle
on the wall
oh she says are you against nuclear weapons?

To Hell with this. Baby or no baby.
Yes I says. Yes yes yes.
I'd like this baby to live in a nuclear free environment

Oh. Her eyes light up.
I'm all for peace myself she says
and sits down for another cup of coffee

7

Maybe that's why I don't like
all this talk about her being black
I brought her up as my own
as I would any other child
colour matters to the nutters
but she says my daughter says
it matters to her

I suppose there would have been things
I couldn't understand with any child
we knew she was coloured

they told us they had no babies at first
and I chanced it didn't matter what colour it was
and they said *oh well are you sure
in that case we have a baby for you*
to think she wasn't even thought of as a baby
my baby, my baby

* * *

We're practising for the school show
I'm trying to do the Cha Cha and the Black Bottom
but I can't get the steps right
my right foot's left and my left foot's right
my teacher shouts from the bottom
of the class Come on, show

us what you can do I thought
you people had it in your blood
my skin is hot as burning coal
like that time she said Darkies are like coal
in front of the whole class – my blood
what does she mean. I thought

she'd stopped all that after the last time
my dad talked to her on parents' night
the other kids are alright till she starts
my feet step out of time, my heart starts
to miss beats like when I can't sleep at night
What is in My Blood? The bell rings, it is time.

* * *

On my bedroom wall is a big poster
of Angela Davis who is in prison
right now for nothing at all
except she wouldn't put up with stuff.
My mum says she is *only* 26
which seems really old to me
but my mum says it is young
just imagine, she says, being on
America's Ten Most Wanted People's List at 26!
I can't.
Angela Davis is the only female person

I've seen (except for a nurse on TV)
who looks like me. She had big hair like mine
that grows out instead of down.
My mum says it's called an *Afro*.
If I could be as brave as her when I get older
I'll be OK.
Last night I kissed her goodnight again
and wondered if she could feel the kisses
in prison all the way from Scotland.
Her skin is the same too you know.
I can see my skin is that colour
but most of the time I forget
so sometimes when I look in the mirror
I give myself a bit of a shock
and say to myself *Do you really look like this?*
as if I'm somebody else. I wonder if she does that.
I don't believe she killed anybody.
It is all a load of phoney lies.
My dad says it's a set up.
I asked him if she'll get the electric chair
like them Roseberries he was telling me about.
No he says the world is on her side.
Well how come she's in there then I thinks
I worry she's going to get the chair.
I worry she's worrying about the chair.
My dad says she'll be putting on a brave face.
He brought me a badge home which I wore
to school. It says FREE ANGELA DAVIS
And all my pals says 'Who's she?'

RODDY LUMSDEN

Prayer to be with Mercurial Women

Let me never have her father
Call me, saying how's about
A round of golf? Instead I'll take
The grim, forbidding monster
Who inspects me for a crooked
Trouser crease. And spare me too
From palmy evenings which sail by
In restaurants, on barstools,
Without a storming off or two.
'Darling, you were made for me,'
I pray I'll never hear those words.
I need to feel I'm stealing
Love another man would kill for.
When in sleep she curls herself
Around me, may she whisper names
That are not mine. I'd prefer
To be the second best she's had.
A curse on mouths which dovetail
As if there'd been a blueprint made,
I'd rather blush and slobber.
And once a month, please let me be
A punchbag. I'll take the blame
For everything: I want to taste
The stinging of a good slap.
I hope I'll find my begging notes
Crumpled, torn in half, unread,
And when I phone, I want to hear
An endless sound of ringing.
Help me avoid the kind of girl
Who means things when she says them,
Unless she's screeching, telling me
Exactly what I am. Amen.

The Bedroom at Arles

(after Van Gogh's painting)

He filled up a cracked glass with hot water from the blue terrine.
Somewhere behind him, all his enemies were arranging a party.
He held the glass high up to his eyes, looking.
The voices in the floorboards had stopped for a while, so he painted.
'When Paul comes, I will show him the garden from indoors.'
Occasional figments of reality bothered the honeycomb walls.
There was a chair for him and a chair for Paul,
There was a window for Paul and a mirror for him
So that they could both see outside.
'If it rains we can play at cards.'
Hands combing at his beard, he painted the heat out of his brain.
This canvas was a place he could really enter, sleep under.
The palette held like a dirty plate in his tweedy lap.
'When Paul comes . . .'

It was very quiet in the Yellow House, but outside
It was a noise. A noise like people coming, going
A noise like dogs running on sand
A noise like the iron gate swinging
A noise like the wind dancing on the canopies of the shops
A noise like the Place Lamartine which he could not see
Through his blindfold of paint, which he could not hear
Through his crescendo of brushstrokes, which he could not smell
Through the anaesthesia of turpentine.
'When Paul comes, I will hang my Japanese print in the scullery.'
'I shall wear my new cravat.'
Even when the voices in the floorboards came back, they only said,
'A little more orange here, a little more orange there.'

Calendar

January is careful with me, is
    cautious in my cold bed.
February breathes at my shoulder,
    'Get on, get on.'
March hasn't heels to drag, flashes by, is
    wind in a keyhole I won't look through.
April crinkles and unclenches like
    cellophane in my wastepaper basket.
May is a pressure-cooker, gently
    simmering my summer.
June opens my skylight. Out in the garden,
    dancing shirts become my dancing-partners.
July walks me on the beach without a leash,
    mows my lawn and trims my hedge.
August buries me neck-high in shell sand,
    the sea washes into my ears.
September is the last step off an escalator,
    though afraid, I must take it.
October's moon is my rucksack. I carry it
    through leaves and the night sky rubs my eyes.
November is the out of focus, out of season
    holiday snap I'd forgotten I'd taken.
December sends me home, unpacks my case
    and blows all my ill winds away.
And January is cautious with me, is
    careful in my cold bed.

Harpooneer

This brink I'm standing on,
Only I believe it's here.
I pull my arm up and out,

Imply the rope. Believe me,
My strong arm's gripped
A foot above the barb.

Look behind me. A cloudless
Sky. The windlass hoards
Half a mile of sleepy rope.

Don't look so frightened.
There are a million targets,
Each with a million points

That the tip might pierce.
Chances are you won't be
The one I haul in tonight.

Chances are I'll be back
Tomorrow, scanning the waves,
Watching, waiting, aiming.

Vanishing

Inside the box, her heels escape the air.
He hears the hollow silence, turns to where
The blades are catching all eyes in the hush.
His click of fingers touches off a rush
Of cymbals. Now he holds the first blade taut
And steers its whetted edge toward the slot.
She slips out of her costume, checks her face
As he reveals the white dove in her place.
She lingers till the last of the applause,
Collects her things, while back on stage he saws
Himself in half with worry, grins with fear.
The sea of faces know she'll re-appear
Amongst them soon. She slams a back-stage door.
Her high heels echo in the corridor.

GLYN MAXWELL

La Brea

Los Angeles. So just
guess what I saw: not the dust
or the wide jammed road, not that. And not
the park where enormous playthings eat

the shouting children. No, and the glass white
televised cathedral? – that
was a sight seen for the sin-
gle flashed moment, and gone.

I saw the tar-pits at La Brea,
where a dark endowed museum squats, and where
the thick blots of lake are watched,
and the haired replicas stroked and touched

by kiddies. There's a tour:
the intelligible stone, the Short-Faced Bear,
the Dire Wolf, American Lion and Mastodon,
and Man with not much brain.

Well they did all make a dumb
choice that day! But my day was warm
and fascinating. Try to see these
tar-pits, at La Brea, in Los Angeles.

Errand Boy

To amble on on the brightening, clouding
pavement to happen to pass whom he wants,
    innocently, to pass involves
passing his home with feigned indifference
and moving on, nowhere left to be heading.

She is the brown bare-armed au pair,
her charges holding her hands. Though he really
    means his major smile at them,
it is all in his own and other way fairly
for her, and their voices are English and clear

as they fade, hers neither as it also fades.
And now he's stuck on an imaginary errand, which
    seems to be suddenly unimportant
from the way he slows down and checks his watch
then monitors interesting forming clouds.

Love Made Yeah

First and zillionth my eyes meet eyes
Unturnable from, unstarable in.
Whoever was marched from the Square of my reason
And to what court, I don't give a hyphen.
    Va t-en to the King!

Our drapeaux are waving and what's in the offing
But tears, tribunals and unwelcome aid?
Nothing but glorious, jealous, incredulous,
Bibulous, fabulous, devil'll-envy-us
    Love made, love made!

Yeah and you say with the press of this planet
Look how it ends up: the heroes felled
In the upshot, the oiliest climb of the customary
Bourgeois fuckers as easy as muttering
    Argent. Ackers. Geld.

Uh-huh, sans doute. But here at the heart
Of the movement I trust my hand in another!
So ABC tell me I'm odds-on to cop it.
That ain't news, guys, I did arrive here
    Via a mother.

No, when the Square is dead again – but
For some oligarchy or puppet or shah,
And I'm banged up and on trial in slippers
For following, wishing on, crediting, catching
    Her my star:

Don't do the pity. Okay, do the pity,
But that won't happen, believe it from me:
Her eyes are as hot as one needs to ignite
The cave in the human guy. I am hers,
    Friends, I am history!

Eyes and Bones on Song

Eyes the Glamourest, Bones the Actor,
adored by millions, admiring none
but self-made equals, moved to the centre
of the studio deepest and bluest, and laughed as
    the spots came on.

They were super-powered, they lit a country
in its dazzled age, when nobody didn't
believe in reward for riches, and nobodies
upped and applauded the winner and marched as
    they ended second.

There was only a chair and a sofa. The floor
was spotless but for a cameraman.
Up high where the wires made one thing clear
enormous sheets of superstars gleamed as
    the show began.

Bones the Actor waded in laughter
loving the camera, and when cool Eyes
the Glamourest swept in white from the corner,
her blacked eyes dwarfing, the million grinned as
    they saw Bones rise.

On the foaming sofa they toyed with enquiries
from nobody less than a lesser star;
the lovable hazarder of naughty questions
coped, cajoled, an in-joke cracking as
    he went too far.

If you had to choose, really really had to,
Eyes the Glamourest edged the show;
Bones was content to remember his moments
with legends, larger than life, famous as
    him. Dead, though.

But Eyes – a scream when she revealed her real name –
Eyes was on song, how she lasted and clapped!
How half the country was with her in spirit
that night! How the deep blue studio ticked as
    England slept.

Out of the Rain, XXXVII

I was born where I knew no man, nor that
the rain would fall, nor end, nor that a boat

would sail away and none that I knew would follow.
All that I knew are gone, and all

that I know I love and is here and knows it will not
know me tomorrow.

I was born, I know, in a town which never
should have been built where it was, but was,

and I live in this same one next to the sea
where nothing changes but is.

But is that one cloud ever going
to move again, as I bat and believe

it will, or is that the sentence passed?
Time has gone, townspeople, townspeople, time is lost.

STEPHEN SMITH

Letters to Myself

I

A long time since I've been *home*,
keeping abreast of news as best I can:
writing letters, or talking down the phone
to relatives who've stood their ground

on the Shankhill side of the Green Line.
The family's connected sense attenuated
since my mother's side decamped over
the water in the Forties to the War,

eroded further by elimination rounds:
disease and quarrels over Wills.
A feeling that they humour my naivety,
catching me offside, theirs the reality

of living daily in the gun's snug sights.
I have evolved a Popish heresy,
my sympathies half faith, half irony
are a gospel flagrancy to Billy's Boys.

My motives suspected by Aunts to whom
ecumenicity is an anathema.
There allegiances can be described
by knowing the right words to the right songs.

They'd leave the room if I played Kevin Barry
on the stereo. My neutered English vowels
are all wrong; my anecdotes would be exposed
if I went back, going home I'd be a tourist.

II

Uncertain where my prejudices lie,
which is the heart's own country – this
domicile where I draw dole, or that other
borderland I frequently patrol.

I'm going back to make reports:
postcards or airmail bulletins
returned to sender at my home address –
attempts to argue with myself.

A Postcard from Finvoy Street

III

I was brought here in nineteen seventy
in my first suit, to be obedient
to a relic of mortality.

The house was packed. I slept upstairs
between grandparents in the room
above the parlour where the body was.

Loss was communicated to me
by the flowers' odour and the tang
Of bleaching fluids in the house.

The furniture was scrubbed each day
to eradicate the germ of death.
Quiet wrinkled like a noose throughout

the home. The body lay in state, dressed
like an opera star, an orange cummerbund
hiding its paunch, a bowler hat across

its chest. I was spared kissing it,
though saw my mother's lips pucker
for his mouth. I tasted cold.

Those days had a pantomime quality.
I feel now for his wife whose grief was lost
inside the crude hyperbole

of burying that hero of his Lodge.
Dead he still seemed capable of anything,
like getting up and having tea with us.

Twenty years have modified childish fears
but still he looms enormously behind me.
If I had a stake I'd drive it through his heart.

IV

In the Black North where the industrial
country leaks down into Lough Neagh,
the Lords of County Antrim held sway.
My ancestors worked their linen crops,

weaving khaki for the troops in '17,
till *flax lung* bandaged up their breaths.
The climate perfect with its yeasty air
for moistening the brittle cloth.

We drove out from the city in the rain
to trace some relatives, a distaff strain.
Beside the lough, its peat intestines
threw back no mirror image to the sky.

You could sink Sodom and Gomorrah in its depth,
a localised apocalypse that would rate
small mention in the world at large.
I imagined Belfast going down on fire.

First Glance

Two flat feet and asthma saved him for us,
drafted with others not quite whole into
Exempted Services, he spent his war
learning the art of husbandry near Clee.

It's where my Gran first saw him stepping through
a gate of cloud, a strange angel when sun-
light bouncing off the plough struck his face gold.
It was enough to turn her righteous head.

She watched him dropping swiftly down through sheep
and scree. She never lost the sweetness of that glance
through thirty years. When he was dead, her still
green innocence planted a ring of daffs to mark his head.

Ulster Holiday

Hills the night slurred bullied the day,
their dull sinews binding the bay
and all the petty life of eye and soul
inside the prison of a natural bowl.

My relatives kept a summer-house up there
for holidays. Ethnic and three parts bare
it's where they went to practise Gaelic,
to empathise and ape the rural Mick.

Pictures from my album nicely convey
their leisure. Grandad supervising hay
into the cart with business-like concern,
Grandmother spooning tea from a brass urn.

They brought their prejudices up with them,
accumulated from a string of men
with managerial nous and control;
experienced in Ulster protocol

Grandma kept Fenians on the door-step
while Grandad paid their cheques.
She saw no reason to condone she said
uppity values conned from the dead

they venerated in their rebel songs,
and Priests talked-up in foreign tongues.
Chiefs of the Protestant Ascendancy
they liked the feudal order of dependency

on them. The shop of sense was shut
on this issue. Bias descended like the foot
of night. The hills entrenched their view
of Time's gracious penury and nothing new.

The Ringers

(Ringer is slang for a stolen and re-sprayed car.)

Childhood was a closed state where information
was controlled and innocence maintained by a blind
of concern. We were kept from people who were bad.
Bohemians existed on the fringes of our awareness;

they grew special by declined association –
rough men who called on my father selling
cars, 'Ringers' in my mother's parlance.
For a long time my brother and myself

considered this a generic expression
for their disturbance at odd hours on our door-bell.
The days after their visits my father
would be shut in his workshop with spray cans,

only appearing to eat. They developed
a fabulous status, something akin
to Wise Men, by virtue of the gifts
their journeys conveyed to us. Just as we

grew used to trinkets bought with their gold
their midnight arrivals ceased. We decamped
shortly after into Wales and the hush money
ended. Now father kept busy with tractors

and the odd day's labour fencing on farms.
We were certain of returning in time
to the *good-life*, little Princes in exile.
It took years to shrug off our innocent burdens.

1992

JILL DAWSON

The Mechanic

Has a little trouble
starting her up this morning.

Rubs his head, says
the distributor cap's
a touch on the wet side;
gets his head
under the bonnet,
tries a bit of
tinkering.

Hmm. Well you see
there could be a
fault in her
starter circuit.
This isn't the first time
he's had to bump it.

Now he thinks he better
try a bigger screwdriver.
Maybe a size 2
would do.

Silken metal
slips between the 2
fixed bolt-heads,
a light sweat is
breaking on his forearms . . .

Such fine forearms,
such a dazzling, varied
toolkit.
How I envy it
and those wild, elegant fingers!

He lights a cigarette,
lingers.

Well he says,
she's ticking over fine now,
good job there was no problem with the
   petrol pipe
(winks, says he could have

lashed it together somehow
a bodge-it-up-get-us-home-job).

He doesn't wear glasses   bury his head in books
not the type I always imagined   not really my type at all,
but such
      skill with his hands such
      patience, perseverance,
      he likes to
      get his hands greasy,
      he likes to
      push until he gets it right.

      Only ever has trouble
         starting her up
         sometimes
         cold mornings

            she needs his
                    touch.

Arrina

I feel his thigh
shift mine
I feel bone beneath skin
stronger than the wind
that shifts the rain
in sheets across the mountains.
I feel his feathered skin
softer than
the splash yellow underbelly
of the wagtail we saw
that day by the water.

He is leaving
at the end of summer.

We will never go back
to the tigered rocks
to the heathered cliffs

I will remember
only
the cloud-white
catch of wool
where a sheep
passed a twig

and how the wind
   moved it

The Devil

I was hungry
He fed me
fish and okra
and rice with coconut

I was thirsty
He gave me Guinness
and bade me drink

I was lonely
He laid down beside me
but I had not come
for that

I had come
to hear him speak
and so he did

He said:
when I knew what it was
that I wanted
I would get it
(For Jah tell we that)
Meanwhile
not to rush
I was young still
Eat my okra
it was good for me
. . . and stay awhile . . .

It was dark and rainy
    late Sunday
and steamy in his kitchen

We had not seen each other
in some time

Lord, I was tempted
to do as he begged me
run away with him
abandon
     everything

For My Sister

I would give you
kind men with pierced ears,
and senses of humour
as wide as their grins,
and sexy

you can have
pramfuls of spindly boys
in Spiderman vests and pants
if you're sure you want them;
a cottage on the eyelid of a cliff
your dreams sealed in gum-pink shells
and furnishing your house . . .

step down to the beach
here is a fishing boat,
battered blue, salt-smelly
and brimming with Marge Piercy books
(I'll waive my principles,
I won't question what you want).

I'll give you hair to your waist
and coltish, a lifetime's supply
of henna;

the cries of the seagulls
the rain fierce as vinegar
hissing in the Devil's frying pan

I'll lay shells at your feet like the sea
and when you open them
out will spout pearls,
in a burst, and wishes.

Paean

  to my child
with his tiny
pod of a penis

O, how I love to
smother it in kisses,
douse it in vanilla talc;
that butter-pale catkin
of downy-soft skin.

His clear yellow urine
– I'm not taking the piss –
only meaning to praise:
    smallness
    friendliness.

O, at last, to love
not to envy it
– which has deflowered no one
penetrated nothing, caused
no more offence than
a chipolata sausage. Uncooked.

To think, all were button mushrooms once
all were sweet and temperate:
Such monuments I would make to it!
The Buds of Stonehenge,
Cleopatra's Thimble,
the Eiffel Thumb.

O, but how my son
will curse me, at twenty
reading this.
So proud will he be
Of his grown-up
    penis.

HUGH DUNKERLEY

Swift Mockery

Swifts flicker,
a sudden formation overhead,
the indefatigable aerobats
glimpsed for an instant,
each bird trailing a rasping scream
still hitting the walls
seconds into its absence

The place settles back;
frantic starlings thrashing
luminous wings,
fighting to gain the rooftops,
the Fred Astaire swallows
capering under the eaves,
crowding the air like insects.

Then a second attack,
a ruddering dash,
the frail furnace of a single bird
blackening into sight,
skimming the housefront,
a sprinting mockery
of the other bird's flight

And the starlings are in a lather,
a hissing fury,
one bird lumbering after the intruder,
hopelessly unwieldy,
the black gymnast already gone,
a high circling speck,
a fine scream thinning to nothing.

Geese

Suddenly there was a white presence
in the garden,
something that could be stoked into a fury,
a hoarse, big-winged beating.

We gave it space, tightening our lives
to allow for what god or demon
had settled in the orchard;

now snatching at windfalls
with six snakelike necks.

At other times it could be
silent and grave,
a fleet of small white galleons.

The Sea Skater

The land recedes,
a dark line thinning
from the corner of each eye.

A lone vertical, he moves
across the sea's welded surface,
his skates etching a wake

on the glass calm, on the
diamond absence of the air,

his breath condensing
in long white chains,
freezing and disintegrating.

Hours ago, the others
fell back, their shouts
dwindling to insignificance,

a fine thread of the familiar
following after him,
then finally snapping.

Now the sky is birdless;
a featureless pewter,
it encircles him everywhere,

a single focus
on which the skylines rotate.

In this uniform glare
there is nothing to sustain the eye,
the mind's clamourings for restrictions;

only the horizons
as they relentlessly migrate.

River

The whole thing is always slipping away
    downstream,
its sliding surface a welter of accelerations
    and sudden brakings,
of whirlpooling gullets.

Where the water rides roughshod over stones,
    sunken trees,
it roughens in foaming reversals,
flows upstream like another river,
    tussling with the current.

Whatever debris is bodied downstream,
    unweighted by the water's uplift,
is laved in the seamless swimming,
is turned and spun by watery hands.

Water boils at the legs of bridges,
is torn and maddened by boulders,
slides over weirs and shatters,
    thundering its applause.

CHRISTOPHER GREENHALGH

Coffee-Break

Half-expecting a tentacle to come up
from the sink's underworld of gunge
and grab me, I gingerly immerse
my hand to search for a spoon,

breaking from the work on my play –
so far there's the watery-eyed son
of a lens grinder, a woman whose
handshake transmits an electric shock,

a circus equestrienne, an Elvis impersonator,
a double-chinned hunchback, a census
enumerator, and an American lady – a Humanist
ruled by the right hemisphere of her brain:

'More people today are reading *King Lear*, and
as a result are having fewer children!'
and 'Making love to you was like seeing
the movie after reading the book!'

There is no plot but it hangs together
somehow like the *Bostik*, poinsettias,
demijohns and half-jar of Vick that
seem an established part of the sill.

Islands

The day no heavier than Spanish poetry,
                          all temperature and colour;
a jet cuts across blue sky with the exactitude
of a diamond scratching glass.

'Something as mundane as the colour of a room
can affect my mood . . .'
something not quite right like a painting maddeningly
off-centre or the cicadas missing a
beat
     and examining the line of masts
in the harbour, the road that curves
around the island like a smile,
the wrinkle of gulls above a tilting horizon,
it's plain that what is
                        'not quite right'
is that you are in Ireland and I am in Greece
watching a cargo of fruit winched ashore –
oranges, nectarines, hirsute peaches
blushing at their obstetric creases
while a girl that might be you
sits precariously on one of the wharf's
carious stumps, a line of salt across her
espadrilles, a languid hand shifting the hair
that drifts across her cheek with the breeze.

From Here and Now

Athens has many ancient ruins
and no car-parks
the traffic all horn
and no brakes.

In a region vulnerable
to earthquakes
I always take the stairs
never the elevator.

The pent-up tensions of
a record heat-wave
crack nerve-ends
of lightning round the city

like a sea-line on
an inky Mercator.
My Walkman headset
figures an Omega,

and like a film that
goes from colour
to black and white
for effect, the

electricity shuts off.
A mosquito
buzzes like a shaver
in a dodgy socket.

I lay out the
contents of
my suitcase like
an haruspex.

Stealing the Mona Lisa

What's there to tell? A garlicky moon.
A suitcase. You squeezing through the window-frame.
The lemonstain headlamps of the Citroën
chamfering the walls of your parents' bedroom
before melting into the night.

The Night I Met Marilyn

'Ask not what your country can do for you, but what
you can do for your country.'

J.F. Kennedy

The night I met Marilyn it was raining
for I remember her shaking her hair free from
a scarf and seeing the donkey-derby of raindrops
fall from her fringe
                and that pampered animality
in response to the cold – part come-on, part disdain,
the dangerously volcanic glamour of a mouth that lured
you to the lip and caused you to fall in.

She had us all mesmerised, resembling a stack
of televisions in an electrical store
all receiving the same programme,
yet behind all the brio, the insouciance,
the gloved white finger quizzical against her chin,
it was obvious – to me anyway – there lay
a nervy vulnerability, a quiet centre of hurt,
and I remember that as she looked at me
she seemed to understand that I understood.

I registered in her a terrible need for love, and
what happened later that evening I have never related.
I promised Marilyn that in her all-too-public life
the privacies that we, at least, shared
                              would be respected . . .

Then that last catastrophic August night:
coming home, I heard the phone insistent behind
the locked door. By the time I had found the key
and made a grab for the receiver, the phone was dead.

It is a painful, intractable thought, and one which
I have kept secret until now, almost thirty years later.

I will say no more, other than that the oblique
details and veiled portrait of the woman I knew
and understood – feisty, ardent, marketable –
can be found in the eponymous heroine of
my latest novel, *Marilyn Runmoe*, published tomorrow:
hardback £16.99, paperback £7.99 with 20 b/w photos.

MARITA MADDAH

Airborne

Suddenly, superbly, she slips –
her legs give way
and magically she tumbles out,
arms flapping, into the sky.
Nothing can hold her
– though the rushing air
sucks at her clothes and hair,
it cannot stop her:
she is airborne, free and strong
as nothing ever was!

And now she shrinks with a shock to size of a pea.
In an instant she can see around her nose,
her lips feel heavier but are easier to close,
her waist is closer to her feet
and her chin slips down three rungs of spine:
she is completely tiny,
batting through the air.

The liquid ball of sun, spilling quietly into its
green forest,
seems so near, it takes her breath.
The sounds of town float up to her
as if they were hot air balloons, quivering.

Her feet tucked up, her chin tucked in,
she tilts her face towards the forest and swoops:
from a height she imagines
she'll brush her belly on the fir tree tips,
as she passes   smooth and fast   just
skim the mantle like a flint.
Now the wood sweeps upwards
massive as a grin – they will collide!

But she slips like a bead
straight through the green
to find her feet press a bed of spongy needles,
dry, sweet-smelling, fine.

Our Brother

When he left,
There was a hole in our lives.
Mother said it was as if the door was left wide open,
Letting the Bay leaves blow into the vestibule.
It was the end of the Summer '79.
The golden days of our revolution
Were waning.

The moon shone hollow-faced at night
(We'd stopped sleeping on the roof
Under the stars: when he left,
It seemed gratuitous. First Attah, then Farzaneh
Took their bedding with them,
Then we all went down into the bedrooms).

Father stopped urging us to pray.
He woke early and performed his ablutions quietly, alone.
His stoop became more noticeable.
He listened to our rages against the 'temporary' government
Now like an old man.
(The army had by this time
Taken our guns and started up
The propaganda against the Left).

Winter crept in through our half-conversations,
Our silent mealtimes.
The sun slunk close to the town's horizon.
Our Bay bent and shone darkly under the heavy sheets of
    rain.

Then one day four men came
To tell us he'd been taken by the army.
They looked clean like Communists.
We trusted their story because they looked simple.

Mother's voice asked which prison,
And they all looked at each other
And the tallest man looked in her face.
And we knew then
He was gone.
They'd hung him in the outskirts
With thirty-eight others,
As an example to those of us
Who thought we could free ourselves.

Even still
Mother watches me shave my face and cries. I hold
Her dry brown hands in conversation frequently.
It is a habit.
We help her with the housework
As we never thought to before.

Father is never in the house now.
He doesn't look me in the eyes anymore.

The Sunflowers

In those long days of thirst
When the dust was turned
And laid upon our skin to cool us,
To keep the heat from damaging us permanently,
In those long dry days
When the shadow of a post
Thin as a needle
Might save us for a moment
From the hell
Of having our heads
Burst open by the light
Like ripened gourds,
In those times
When we children
Grew
Too tired to brush the flies away
But let them settle on our cracking lips
A woman grew some sunflowers:

Impractical,
Wrong-headed,
That watched the great god
Gormlessly all day.
All day gazed lovingly into its
Incapacitating glare,
Admitting fatigue
Only after sundown,
When their golden faces
Dropped suddenly, puzzled.

Planted in amongst the strict brown ruts
Of edible vegetation,
Taking more than their fair share
Of goodness from the soil,
They brought nothing –
Not even drops of oil from their mouths

That sucked the air relentlessly,
Yet selflessly,
Following the antics of their white inimical god.

Glorious and yellow,
Meaning nothing.
Empty vessels,
Feeding nothing,
But eyes.

Song for Ali Tiko

Ali Tiko, are you dead now?
Sometimes I think you must be.
What was that dress you wore?
The powder on your face was flour?

Somewhere you might live
Thousands of miles away,
Hundreds of years away,
Scraping your dust for roots.

Ali Tiko, have you children?
Remember Raasa Guba?
Are you in Raasa Guba?

As kids we'd ape the mad baboons,
Throw rocks at them and scold them,
Laugh at Daniel hiding from them,
Older than us and hiding,
Singing,
>'Daniel *phud* dora
>Daniel *phud* dora
>Daniel's a chicken
>Daniel's a chicken . . .'

The sun white
The dust white
The heat swimming about in our dark heads.
Seeking out the shadows
Always seeking out the shadows,
Pressing backs
Flat against the mudwalls
To have our feet in shade,
Yours shoeless in the tin roof's shade.

Ali Tiko,
Toothless,
Grinning,
Shy,
Carrying the jamjar,
Smaller than me,
Poorer than me,
Following my stubborn walk across the compound,
Scratched and scorched across the grassland,
My jamjar for the grasshoppers
Swinging on a string that scored a line into your fingers,
Little Ali Tiko.

Easy to catch,
The grasshoppers, bright green
Against the grasses. Dry as grass,
Rasping dry as grass, but green,
So green.

Unready for this drought.

Blood for Rain

Her scream as falling down the well
She hit the walls in blackness
Was the scarlet shriek of skin torn jagged from the bone.

They knew that well,
And heard that though
The first long drop of neck was narrow,
Eventually it swelled
So that its slimy walls curved outwards,
And in again to meet the ragged bottom of its basin.

There was no water to be had there.

All afternoon her crying never stopped.
The sun stole strangely white across the hill.
Snakes were silent under rock.

There was nothing they could do.

In the evening when her long dark groans rose thinly from
                                                  the hole,
They knew the child was being born
And so the drums began.

Her husband who was just a boy,
Stuffed his hands into his mouth and chewed.
The women rocked and wailed dark as rocks into the dawn.

And then it started:
Spot in darkening spot, the rain came,
Lifting off the dust in skins.

There was no sound but
The rain
Suddenly down
All over Raasa Guba.

STUART PATERSON

Sandend 1989

There should have been haddock,
Herring, grayling, salt-barrels,
Sharp knives and the sticking
Of soaked woollen jumpers
And loose floral dresses,
A busied throng by the harbour,
And scaled mesh, stinking tails
And heads for the shrieking cloud
Above and all that was there
Was a rotted line round a green mooring-post
And an empty sky overhanging a swell
No longer fit to yield.

Gigha

There is a cottage
Sitting low on a brae for me,
Its thick white walls
A curse to wind, its slate roof
Hermetic, stout rowan door,
Quivered grain for a rap, mine
In the howl of Tarbert's storm.
A log on the fire is mine
To turn, a malt
On the mantelpiece for you.

Heather springs a swirl
Nine inches from the wall
The whole way round,
A bloom and a soft reed
To wake me each morning,
No rabbits gather underneath
The lintel while I'm gone.
There are thick patched blankets
On an old wooden bed
And a shillelagh by the range
To greet my enemies.

This is Gigha,
Its sea-pebbled path
Not a gull's cry away
From here.

Garrier at Midnight

(The Garrier is a stream flowing down from the Fenwick Moors
in Ayrshire, through several of the county's villages, one of
which is Kilmaurs.)

'Kilmaurs.' It was a midnight walk
Inspired by Whitman at an ungodly hour,
Torch ploughing the back roads, a huge dark pall
Stretching away from the beam to who-knew-where,
Lighting a soft-rimmed amber over the hedges;
Scattering strange eyes, we felt like gnats
On the edge of God's holy cave.
Past Jocksthorn, onto the Fenwick Road,
Past the old church, onto the Soldier's Park
To the murmured pull of the Garrier;
Bridged by a night-world, then,
We stopped, lit up and spoke, hushed,
Of open spaces and big skies, mountains
Soft and towering above. Intrigued
By what went on below, before
The day recalled its flow, we shone
A light on Grandfather Garrier, cooled
In the linens of cardboard, tin and wire,
Broken-backed by boxes, soft-cut trees and tyres,
Bed-stones for a new century here.
There, slither-still by a toppled rock,
Hung an eel, a fine foot at least he was,
Seeing no mountains above, suns, jet-streams
Or new shores, his sky marked only by
A fag-end or skater, underlings, live or dead, to him.
Were we gods to this traveller, even if he saw us,
Or shadows on a perfect horizon?
His wild smoothness eating our glare
Disturbed our way and, later, passing by Tour,
He hung in the mind, his brilliant blindness
Seemed huge, a proud unnerving stare.

Shroud

These leaves stuck to your shoe-sole
Are crushed moths,
Blind flutterings caught underfoot.
And this stem of grass placed
Behind your ear is a fossil,
A badge of lifelessness
Brown and dried, curled
To the contours of your skin,
A corpse on a mortuary slab.
These flakes of skindrift
On the carpet fell slowly,
Dead wingless flies in an ashen pile.
And the mud-splashes circling the hem
Of your jeans have hardened,
Faded to dull copper
And begun to crack and peel.

Sap runs from your nostrils,
The bent back shouldering the northern winds,
And drops in sinewed rivulets
To your jacket front,
Residue of a bright but broken thing.

Each year your shuffle shortens
With the reddening of the moons,
And some more of the world
Is drawn to you, preparing you
As you hoard your dying round you
Like a shroud.

Silversmith

Down by the loch, an osprey dove
To his mirror, vain and hungry lord
Of waters not yet spoiled by cove
And bay. The feeding of a bird

Such as he is somehow holy
To this slow and satiated
Tourist in the grim land, lonely
For the wild heart, how he waited

Months and years to see this great sight
Burst the blue with vision free of
Greed or malice, twisting tight
The wind, which asks 'Can this be of

The winged, the hoofed, the small below
Of air, water, worldless spaces?
Beside this lord, the light is slow,
Fell the wind which wins his races.'

A world struggles in his grasping
Talons, bars to shackle weakness,
Last breath stolen by the rasping
Rushing passage, silver meekness

Flying different skies. His vision
Holds the continents and passes
Through the moons, a winged collision
Shadowing the silvered masses.

STUART PICKFORD

Over a Foreign Land

(Kew Gardens, London)

The jokes are obvious: all those pricks
(Some girls are in a scrum of giggles);
Is it cacti or cactuses like buses?;

John Wayne. But below the patter
A silence grips, though the itch
To touch is furtively licensed. Looking

At the rubbery shapes our language
Slips, is outgrown, can't be used
As pins. Words are shadows moving

Over a foreign land. Cacti won't do
For cucumbers, corals, cabbages, they're
Stitched leather, a furry ball, a fin.

Those who call everything A Spade
Gradually become smart talkers, excited.
(We are Eskimos with ten words for snow.)

Our silence slackens, we possess the cacti,
Are comfortable again, moving to
The Alpine House's small, suburban plants.

They are pretty, nothing too much
Or too memorable. They demand nothing
And one word nets them all.

mother finally told the facts of her son's suicide

came
his head on
to the railway line

soon the train
placed he the rail
walked he

it was was it
a evening tuesday the march of month

came the train soon
his head on he placed
to the railway line he walked

soon the train soon
he placed the rail the rail
he walked to the railway

a evening tuesday it was
the march of month it was

the train soon came the train soon the train
he placed his head on he placed he placed
he walked to the railway he walked he walked

soon soon the train soon
the rail he placed the rail the rail
he walked he walked to the railway

a tuesday evening it was
the month of march it was

the train soon came
he placed his head on
he walked to the railway line

the train soon
he placed the rail
he walked to the railway

it was a tuesday evening
it was the month of march

the train soon came
he placed his head on the rail
he walked to the railway line
it was a tuesday evening
it was the month of march

Cutting Dad's Nails

Like wrestlers, your left arm locked
Under mine, I'd clip your nails. Mum
Was no bloody good: unimpressed,
Like when she sorted out whinging kids.

You would squirm and Jesus Christ
Before flicking away the oily grime
Stubbed to the hilt of each nail,
Blunt, and yellow as your nicotine fingers.

The size of your hands was frightening:
Each an unclenched fist, slashed
With coal scars; the broad palms
Muscled with calluses, like the balls of my feet.

Pen-pusher, bookworm, I'd never
Done a real day's work. You
Thumbed each white finger-tip,
I had woman's hands, you joked,

I think. But I never saw the blood
On the coal or picked my mate
From the cutting machine or took the crap
On every building site. And coped.

So when you wormed and pulled back
Your little finger as if burned and clamped
It sharpish under your arm, I smiled
And loved it and could be your son.

Port le Grand

Sun squatted doggedly
On the long afternoon road
Wet with heat haze.
The chain purred.
The distance's smoothed hills
And charcoal-suggested trees
Stood like theatre scenery,
Robbed of their third dimension.
A combine paddled through
The barley's watery surface,
Laying roads of silent bristle. Sliding
Into a stone-baked square, turned
On the edge of a second,
The world is made fresh –
Port le Grand!

> We had made a lunch here
> In a pool of trembling shade . . .
> A melon, a sliced harvest moon,
> Rocked itself in being halved; oozing
> Cheeses and a nutty cob;
> Plums and peaches,
> Silky, creamy tissues
> Lusciously yellowed through by sun.
> A bird sang our happiness
> While plodding across her yard
> A woman cradled an urn.
> The world gathered around us
> And was ours.

A wood pigeon rehearses his three dry notes
And I catch myself here again.
A tractor slowly stammers past,
Bright packages of hay
Wobbling towards a ruinous barn.
There is a permeating joy here

Seeping in as when spring unfolds,
Not just from revisiting what is known
But reliving what was forgotten
And tasting it all again:
Crisp, vigorous and cool.

Surrealism

(Based on a trip to the Leeds City Art Gallery Exhibition)

Like goldfish against the glass you
Confront 'Mediterranean Bird with Cat Foetus'.
Your prejudices tremble, shake, burst:
'What's that un? I could do that.'

This world is punctured, folds in
On itself; our reality haemorrhages, ideas
Fall like dominoes; words decay on objects,
Unpeel themselves like old paint.

Stripped of the mind's scaffold, history's
Blight, the tyranny of habit, the world stands
Bristling, chaotic, raw, while clutching
Questionnaires you search for The Answers,

Sifting the half-corroded shapes dredged
From the mind's floor. Eyeballs bulge
At the windows; 'The' fills the blackboard,
Incomplete possibility, indefinite article.

Screams are locked within bowed heads
While Mr Punch grins and laughs and grins
At the scorpions scuttling over flesh
And ants dripping from melted watches.

This is the dissecting table where we slice
The living coral of the mind, where umbrellas
Meet sewing-machines, where there are
Coils for making cubes of cloud.

Your mind oscillates between worlds
Like an optical illusion. 'It's crazy.
He's on another planet,' you note
With 'Exquisite Corpse', resenting it

Yet sensing its horror tugging towards
The abyss. The sofa-lips of Dali
(Heard of him) appeals more with its 'Kiss
My Arse' humour. Ernst though is weird.

Leaving Leeds, a tap pours 'Benson & Hedges'
Through the fish-bone trees, as you say
It was interesting, liked (coyly) some.
Threading our way home you become confident,

Cocky. And there is Pateley, cupped
In the dale, real, coherent, spinning
Slowly on its local axis beneath
The 'Light Bulb with Tissue Paper' moon.

1993

SEAN BOUSTEAD

To be Continued

Others in the damp alleys played at life
with girls from the roughest schools, or with knives.
If they noticed the sunlight on the leaves
it did not seem to cause them fear.
They lived in details, chip-shops and bus-fares;
I lived in poems by admitted queers.

Only those images I could afford
I packed for the journey out of Salford.
I meant my life to be a metaphor
of high art and damaged lungs.
I meant to burn the books and to snap strings,
to live for beauty and to die quite young.

Nobody watched me, nobody was fooled,
so that the time came when even I failed
the careful loneliness of my dull face.
I drew sticks along a railing,
I watched light shift along a cracked ceiling:
this is a new and inexact feeling

language seems to have expected of me,
the doctor says will be temporary.
When I bid the leaves and the clouds come to me
all the leaves and all the clouds move.
If this is wind, if art, still I have proved
something, and it walks and it looks like love.

Spring

It seems that only when the spring begins
old neighbours fail, die. Death has no surprises –
a house shut and the lawn gone begging,
   young men come, to fix prices –

yet spring astonishes, the spring is so mundane,
so literal. And typical spring sounds – of hoses
nattering at bonnets, till they slacken, pull undone
   from the steel taps in washhouses –

typical spring sounds are cold, echo. From semis
kids – each year seeming much quieter, seeming warned
of something – rush into the promise of summer
   to have rosebud and water wars.

Coming to Fields

The doctors say that I am on the mend,
improved from having too much of lying,
too much of hate and disillusionment.
I have to keep on, they say, keep trying,
it is just a fad, an after-effect,
the way I wish winter to come early,
I must get out more and I must get pissed.
    I must keep hold of facts,
they add, I must dress and eat properly.
I must find work, say the psychologists.

But each day asks of me a downpayment;
I have walked many miles and I still hear
the terrible echo of the pavement.
If I eat something or I fix my hair
I am merely dancing out a half-thought,
shining silently, like newly-cut grass.
I know how terribly this season feels,
    I would make an effort
if seasons weren't so difficult to guess.
I tell no one I've been coming to fields –

they could think of so many better ways
to pass a summer than to sit in fields.
And near the fields there is a motorway.
I tell no one I've been coming to fields,
that the summer fields are my destiny –
broad seas, of brown clay, of burnt stalks of wheat,
mostly of styles of green – silver green, proud
    and honest green, tiny
sheaths of green shimmering in the high heat.
The shadow of a high, cathedral cloud.

Drunken Admirals dancing out of time
to a slight breeze. Wasps, hornets, damsel-flies,
aimless and hasty, rushed lists of first names.

A sweep of sparrows and their dead, bead eyes.
The grace of things, even of the midges
hovering in shadows. Cornflowers, poppies,
petals brilliant in the sun's fierceness,
    harsh and blurred images
of colour; all the flowers, day-trippers
to the sun's violence and fieriness,

to the planned arrogance of the summer.
I tear flowers casually with two fingers,
I am their disciple and redeemer,
they are my entertainers and thinkers.
What faiths could others tell of, that damage
to such easy and indifferent beauty
would seem evil, would become a vile lie?
    My flowers, what am I
that I should not have such pain my duty?
If I wish winter will the summer die?

Mid-Season

We come, out from the lines of cars,
    out from removed, more famous places,
out for the day. And if we care
    about the litter, the seasoned prices,

the habits we have stepped somehow out of,
    suddenly we have forgotten – the air
so clear our lives seem memories, dreams, of
    which the car's a useful souvenir.

We come, and we push around the shops,
    we buy postcards or a lotion
and we pick disappointedly at bags of chips.
    We come. It is an absolution

from the sin of living seriously, fiercely, owning
    things. Soon as wind stirs, then
we turn away from the arcades and awnings,
    push toward the beach, in thin

pulses. All the side-roads are cold, shaded,
    and have salt or fish tastes.
In the backings white vans are being loaded.
    Round each of the road's twists

the light is difficult, sudden; there's a hissing
    sound, the sound, almost of begging,
of the water, water pushing at walls, promising
    difference, different and new days beginning.

One-Way

    Swinton,
  Pendlebury, Clifton; 'Better
Bargains', 'Smoking Kills'; the small shops in the small towns
  similar, predictable, down
to the bicycle leant outside, the sign with a letter

    missing:
  dark bus-windows
only glimpse life, pass by – even people crying, people kissing
  become simplified, things
opened quickly to be seen and then as quickly closed –

    no
  trying to step
off, to find reasons – not the slightest wish to know
  what's happening now,
what exactly it is happening, back at the last stop –

    easier
  to have done,
not at all to know: maybe feeling shameful, feeling lazy;
  maybe thinking, 'Later
someone will explain'; a church, a hospital, a cemetery; Bolton.

ELEANOR BROWN

Pity

It was fully an hour, I think, after you'd gone
When the image arrived at the front of my mind
That had lurked at the back as you talked on and on.

It was summer in Normandy (so far, it's kind)
It was Wednesday – market day – one narrow street
In a village like any not far from the sea

Where a lobster costs less than a sliver of meat.
    And the oyster-man opened one up for me, free,
        When I said I had never had oysters before,

        And was friendly in French, so I had to pretend
        It was lovely, but thankyou, I wouldn't have more.
Very English, this eagerness not to offend.

At the end of his stall, in their shallow white trays,
Were the crabs. Still alive, of course – guaranteed fresh –
But, all brooding on Fate and the horrible ways

That we have of extracting their tender white flesh,
They were listless as warriors caught fully-armed,
Yet unmanned by the prospect of death at the hands

Of a captor so huge he can never be harmed.
And the claws that had terrorised Normandy's sands
Were now feebly manoeuvred to sign 'I resign.'

Thus, dejected and helpless and lying in heaps,
They exuded a visual kind of a whine,
Like the viscous emission that bubbles and seeps

From a bottle of something unpleasantly thick.
From a crevice – a mouth? – at the front of each shell
Came a bubbling oozing. Not rabid. Not quick.

An occasional pop, a continual well.
Like the stuff we produce when we've cried all we can:
The catarrhal saliva that clings to our lips.

    Like the trickling self-pity that renders a man
      So repulsive our patience first frays and then rips
Altogether – especially after a night

When we've sympathised, soothed and attempted a joke,
And been silent at last, when a silence seemed right.

Dying crabs, you reminded me of, as you spoke.

Bitcherel

You ask what I think of your new acquisition,
And since we are now to be 'friends',
I'll strive to the full to cement my position
With honesty. Dear – it depends.
It depends upon taste, which must not be disputed;
For which of us *does* understand
Why some like their furnishings pallid and muted,
Their cookery wholesome, but bland?
There isn't a *law* that a face should have features –
It's just that they generally *do*;
God couldn't give colour to all of his creatures,
And only gave wit to a few;
I'm sure she has qualities, much underrated,
That compensate amply for this –
Along with a charm that is so understated
It's easy for people to miss.
And if there are some who choose clothing to flatter
What beauties they think they possess,
When what's underneath has no shape, does it matter
If there is no shape to the dress?
It's not that I think she is *boring*, precisely –
That isn't the word I would choose:
I know there are men who like girls who talk nicely,
And always wear sensible shoes.
It's not that I think she is vapid and silly;
It's not that her voice makes me wince –
But chilli con carne without any chilli
Is only a plateful of mince . . .

Sonnets

II

I laugh in climax, and you ask me why
(jaws locked around my loosened consciousness,
as though at such a time I might be less
inclined to weigh my words, or tell a lie –
and I appreciate it's worth a try).
So, let me catch my breath, and somewhat after,
explain that climax, more or less, is laughter.
An answer not designed to satisfy;
darkly displeased, you'd like it more if I
called out, or gasped, invoked my banished God?
Which suppositions all receive a nod:
'I'd like to see you angry. Make you cry.'
A few cold words? Cheap tears? You should be much
more flattered that my laugh rewards your touch.

III

You ask what brought me here – into your bed! –
Last-ditch attempt to find myself elsewhere
than in the narrow cloister of my head.
Apartheid-victim – as you stroke my hair,
as you caress the curve from waist to hip,
and even as we kiss, some splintered part
of me is waiting for me, with a whip . . .
don't ask what brought me here. Where would I start,
to find the language for an honest answer?
Better you should assume my appetite
Led me to you, as music draws a dancer;
better you should assume there was no fight.
      Revolt against my segregated mind.
      Lust for oblivion. Which I do not find.

VII

Conscious of some discomfort recently,
unable to identify the cause –
not headache, hunger, nothing I could see –
I put myself away behind closed doors,
and tested gingerly all areas
that might be harbouring the irritant.
On being satisfied that various
organs and limbs betrayed no element
of bruising or disease, I hawked and spat
to clear my throat: and, with a tinny sound,
the phrase 'I love him' clattered to the ground.

      Stuck in my throat and choking me. Just that
Small, three-edged piece of shrapnel from the fight
between my reason and my appetite.

X

One kiss to open; one to set the seal.
And in between, of course, kisses in their
Catullan thousands. One, first, to invite,
accept, affirm, and breed desire for more;
one a full-stop – in showing you the door.
One eloquent, establishing the right
to trace your jawline, stray into your hair;
one taciturn – no rights, no tongues, no deal.
One trembling and expectant, through a smile;
one firmer and unyielding, through a wall
made of decisions made beyond recall.
One to say, 'I am yours now, for a while';
one, 'I am *not* yours now. But I have been.'
And in between? Oh, God – and in between.

XI

It makes me wonder what you had in mind;
what personal, exclusive cruelty
you were devising, sweetheart, just for me.
Would it have been exquisite and refined?
Or wholesale and obliterating? An
ecstasy of humiliation, or
basic brutality? Me, on the floor,
begging as only broken women can?
      I'm not entirely ignorant of violence.
I never learned to like it – but I know
what happens when the vitriolic flow
of insults chokes itself into a silence.
      My last love taught me how to dodge a fist.
You could have tried to hurt me. You'd have missed.

XIV

Tonight ingenuous and generous
oblivious desirable forgiving
also imperative and dangerous
and burning steadily in love with living
sweet-limbed bright-eyed smooth-skinned and crimson-lipped
heady as conversation over drink
also inconsequential having slipped
out of the reach of conscience and I think
perhaps remorseless certainly no more
than ever willing to forgo the right
to laugh looking for somebody to pour
this brilliance over o I am tonight
young lovely insolent and flown with wine
and this might all be yours. If you were mine.

XVI

Just the touch of your fingers upon mine
(lighting a cigarette) and I have been,
just for a moment – anyway – a queen,
only a moment – just the space a line
might do for the expression of – and yet,
recalling how your hand was cupped around
my own – and the inevitable sound
of my breath changing – and my cigarette
not being very steady – I must be
conscious of this: that lecture as I may
'This thing is *over*', there will come a day
when you – perhaps in boredom – reach for me,
and I, though full of frigid wisdom now,
will know I should refuse, but not know how.

TRACEY HERD

Artifice

It was no wild landscape; merely
a frost-pinched narrow lane
making its deliberate way
between fields and the back
walls of gardens, the sun
set at its late morning slant.
Primly it sat like an ornament
on its dustless mantelpiece, or
a photograph of a mirthless
child. Everything seemed
to be exactly where it should.
I added little flowers of detail
plucked from hidden childhood places:
a mother stiffly pushing an antique
navy-covered pram, on her way home
from coffee with a friend.
She stoops briefly to stroke
a ginger tom, streaked
with more lively shades
of sun. Baby is silent,
fingering a stuffed monkey
on her pillow, sweating under
her layers of wool. The
only sounds are the wheels bumping
over hard packed dirt, and ginger
back on his wall, purring warmly
enough to melt the frost.
He soon lost interest
in the pair as they trundled
out of focus, into a colder,
less assured picture, into
the deep, dark woods, beloved
of fairytales.

Charades

The snow falls on a tiny church,
on a pantomime of headstones:
here lies the wicked witch
who will turn the snow to black ice
and here is the old clown
in faded costume, mouth full of holly berry
and here is the fairy godmother
whose surfeit of good turns couldn't save her
and here is the princess who slashed
her wrists with the shattered slipper
and here is the man who thought he was Christ
blessing the worms, and the rats
that were once the high stepping horses
pulling Cinderella's golden coach.

A Terrible Day

'I'm going to phone the Children's Home.'
My mother's voice was calm
as she sauntered down the stairs.
I rushed down, sliding painfully
on the last few as she lifted
the cream-coloured receiver,
silencing the dialling tone
with a twist of her sharp finger.

'Hello, is that the Children's Home?
I'm so sorry to bother you. I've phoned before,
about my daughter.'

She walked past me in the hall
back up the newly carpeted stairs.
I screamed and sobbed
to shut out the noise
of the cheap vanity case
scraping down from the loft.
Then how I humbled myself,

trying to get her attention, on my knees
tugging at her skirt
as she swatted me easily away,
like a Queen, reluctant
to dispense her pardons, but finally
would come (a little later each time)
the generous gesture.

The clothes would be carefully replaced
in their various drawers
and the lady in charge
of the home would be informed.
'I'm sorry to have put you
to so much trouble.'

When my father came in
from work, he would ignore me
and go straight to mother,
careful to step on the newspaper
and not the freshly scrubbed linoleum.
'You must have had a terrible day
darling.' (I always wondered how he knew)
'Sit down and tell me about it.'

The Cage

Sitting at opposite sides
of the table, we circle
each other warily,
weary from the acrobatics
of our quarrel.

In my mind, on a surface
of sawdust, under bright lights,
two dogs jump
through blazing hoops
towards each other.
In reality, we sit quietly,
our cigarettes balanced
like guns in the ashtray:
one flick of my finger
and I'd blow you away.

My words crack. You're
the ringmaster's horse
shying away: advantage me.
You stumble forward
onto your knees,
your bony muzzle, inches
from the whip. I want
to strike out till you squeal
with pain, so the tears come
and release me from
this cage, to hold you
in my arms again.

Marilyn Climbs Out of the Pool

He made her do the same scene
fifty times. Flashbulbs
light up her face
as she slips in and out
of the water with barely
a wrinkle of blue.

The cameras light up the pool
like bursts of applause.
Again and again she smiles
making hard work of it all,
bringing one glistening limb
right out of the water.
Her toes reach for the concrete edge;
fair hair curves damply over one
bare shoulder. Her eyes are
the colours of the water, night
blue with silver darting
frantically in every direction.

A Searching Pace

The horses batter round: well
muscled, half a ton
crushing grass stalk down.
Their hooves spit stone,
enticed by whip and the crowd's
dark roar. Dig down

beyond the chest's thick bone
and damp, coarse hair.
Dig down. The black runner
pitches over, in a blur
of stick and brush;
his flailing finish premature:

the bursting heart, bright
as silks, fluttering briefly
as his rivals take repeated flight.

JOEL LANE

The Silent Majority

Behind a barred window and a padlocked door
he'd made a private chamber of echoes.
From the radio station, painted like a schoolroom
in green, he broadcast old records and chatter
to the staff and patients of an asylum.

It gave him a place to be himself,
somewhere to bring his friends, to be heard
and not seen. It gave him voices
for all the aching moments: shelved
in the raw archive of past songs.

He could call on a thousand dry throats,
hearts worn on numbered cardboard sleeves,
dry eyes and dusty stumbling tracks
and Dusty Springfield – the old traumas
that he mimed as the records played.

Between tracks, he'd always ask
the listeners to phone the station's number
with their dedications or requests.
Nobody ever rang. Off microphone
he swore at his mute audience:

'Talk to me, you bastards!'
His face changed from mock anger
to real unease, as much lost then
as he was at home. I thought
of de la Mare's 'one man left awake'.

He locked up the station in darkness,
and we passed through the stone arch
and the hospital grounds, held back

from the road by high spiked railings.
We waited, feeling cold, in a bus shelter

whose glass was splintered on the pavement.
Across the main road, some black houses
stood behind an acre of waste ground;
at our backs, the Victorian hospital buildings
kept their people shut up and shut off.

Engaged

You're talking slate. Chalk couldn't mark
its tacky slope. You're talking hailstones
spattered against all the small panes
on the outside of this telephone box.

You're talking spider's web, too thin
to catch anything but the lamplight.
Your voice scratches and won't retract
even if I hang up and walk free.

But if I keep one ear to myself
it's not to beat you to the last word.
I want the fall that the coin made
before you started to talk like this.

Energy and Silence

Above the vacant offices, a thin wind
tears up a flock of starlings like cinders
in the heat-haze over a bonfire.
In the park, the sun's afterimage
burns its way through a shivering jigsaw

of leaves, peeling from a plaster sky.
The stretching of boughs, loosening of tiles,
draws the wind's shape against the night.
It's dark in these rooms. Behind glass.
The space inside us. Do you know

if all these visions are folded up
into the body? The light is stale there,
written over with creases. You can't reclaim
love from the tissues, the tepid fluids;
they don't carry the banner of freedom.

There's energy in materials. Like
the charge on a door handle; or the face
you can rub into a polythene sheet –
like the Turin Shroud, an artefact
held up as a miracle. Surfaces.

Friction. While birds and electric
cables sing, we huddle in back rooms,
passing on rumours about the body
static: it attracts, it stings. But
it has no power. It does no work.

Messages

A friend, passing the hostel one night, threw
gravel at my window to summon me.
Now rain makes the noise of tearing sheets
against the glass; or of trapped wings.
Something wants to escape or break in.

Last week, the gale that made headlines
slammed back an open window and smashed it.
A language student wrote these words,
neatly, in pencil on the kitchen wall:
Mon Dieu, aide moi. Je t'en supplie.

Some drunk on the third floor ran
back and forth in the night, punching
doorframes, shouting *Does he fuck? Does
he fuck?* The fracture of privacy
creates isolation; so do the thefts,

and the rules barring overnight visitors.
It's mid-February; a lack of messages
can hurt. Even when the clouds lift
the light is dispersed, without a focus.
A winged foot has sprained its ankle.

Gravel Tides

He told me how he had taken the last
train to the coast, to watch the tide
go out; he walked miles over the unlit sand,
until his feet were numb, then found a hotel.
'My God, it was cold.' Still, the sea had taken
the harpoon of his fear, and broken it free.
As he spoke, the brick of houses dissolved;
the wind blew inside their frames,
carrying grains of light to his face.

Nothing breaks the gravel skin
of the school playground where children scatter,
crested with urgency. I watch them
through the railings. This tide shrugged
me off, once, still breathing to its pulse,
still with salt in my mouth. From that wall
a girl of eight borrowed a carved face
to tell me: if you don't follow God
you are following the Devil. Now the voices
break in air, almost coherent, like sleet
just before it reaches the window.

Once the walls have been restored,
the scaffolding is removed; those who live
in these buildings cannot see their frames.
No one would think the grey cliffs formed
from the spittle of tides; unless perhaps
they saw the fossils that defaced them,
the fingernails and teeth that we left
embedded, our hostages, in walls
that were more real than we expected.

ANGELA McSEVENEY

Changing a Downie Cover

First: catch your downie.

They're big animals, sleep a lot of the time,
barely stirring as they snooze endlessly
loafing around on the beds.

But they only have to see
a clean cover –

suddenly you have six by three
of feathery incorporeality kicking and screaming
in your hands.

Wrestle them to the floor
and kneel on their necks:
you can't hurt them, no bones to break.

Pushing their head into the bag
keeps them quiet

but you're never sure
till each corner is flush inside the cover
securely buttoned shut.

They give up after that.
Pinioned in floral print polycotton
they lie back down and sleep.

Blacking a Hearth Stone

I kneel
with the floor as an easel,

clean up my dull grey canvas
with a duster and a wet cloth,

I work with just one pigment
charcoal dark.

Back bent with patience
I smooth it on with my fingertips
kneading at the pitted rock.

On rougher parts I work close
with an old nailbrush.

Later it dries
and I buff on a varnished shine
with a soft cloth.

I straighten up, stand back,
admire my Study In Black
framed by an armchair and a pale rug.

Night Shift

I would wake up when I heard Dad
coming in at the front door.

The others slept through his early morning noises:
a toilet flush, one cup of tea boiling.

There seemed no place for him
at home all day Saturday
and most of Sunday.

His skin paled
apart from one weather-beaten patch
at his throat.

'It's no life for a man,' he sometimes grumbled
'this living like a mole.'

During school holidays I made
no noise at home.

Mum went to parents' nights alone.
She was sick of darning where industrial acid
ate away his clothes.

At five o'clock I'd be sent
to waken Dad for tea.

The curtains in my parents' room
were almost always closed.

Woman with Lilac Sash

(Lady Agnew of Lochnaw *c.* 1893 by John Singer Sargent,
1856–1925)

Self-composed Edwardian lady
you sit firm-backed in your period chair.

The broad silk sash winds twice
round a handspan whalebone waist
I don't envy you.

Forever at home to visitors
you keep it formal as we wander past.

You've held this pose for a century
fresh as yesterday
in your endless prime.

What did you think
during all those sittings?

Did convention bend
to let you chat with the artist?

Somewhere Madam
your chaperone still hovers
just outside the frame.

Dark eyes, cool brow,
every raven tress in its place,
you give away nothing but your loveliness.

My Crime

Unlike my brother I did not die young.

I had fits and croup, caused sleepless nights
and trips to clinics.

My feet outgrew shoes which cost money
and I was no beauty.

I answered back, stayed out and was ungrateful.
People washed their hands of me (more than once).

Unlike me my brother died young
golden-haired, one week old, in an incubator.

The Sweep

I heard him singing first at the back of my mind.
My bowed head went on working.

When I did raise my tiring eyes they met his
six storeys up across the way.

Behind the windowpane I drew a breath.
He stepped from one chimney stack to the next
and went on singing.

DERYN REES-JONES

The Ladies

One hand slammed against the faulty lock
we scan messages on doors, chiselled
in biro and succinct
as gravestone epitaphs – that 'men are bastards'
and that 'Sue loves Steve', 'Marie's a slag'
and 'Ann shags anything that moves': assess

the catalogue of rich obscenities, puzzle
the helplines with their numbers
scribbled out: retch
at the blue detergent, pig-shit sweet amidst
incisive twist of toilet paper, and the
niagara flush of the
unfettered toilet chains. It is

no wonder we avoid each other's eyes,
busy with soap and regurgitative roller towels; strange
that next we rearrange ourselves
in mirrors, and then put lipstick on, and,
with sidelong glances,
try on each other's smiles.

The Chair

It might be any Winter, any furnished room –
a table with a tablecloth, a pot-plant in a pot,
my mother's grandmother in charcoal skirts
heating up irons beside the fire, proving
a batch of heavy-headed bread, then
stooping to sit down beside the hearth
absorbed into the scene – the ordinariness
of relief that blends into this strong
domestic scene, the straight-backed kitchen chair.

Those were the childish Winters that I heard about
but never saw – the way she pulled my mother
on her lap to play a guessing game
of scissor, paper, stone – testing
with hands the fleshly certainty of what things
almost are. No photograph could catch it.
Standing alone today the reconstructed room
now smells of lilacs, not the yeasty dough and hints at loss,

the sunlight tightening like a high, bright wound
against the icy and unloving air –
the half-held portions of the past condensed
into an open window, and an empty chair.

First

Like the impossible floodings of a fleet of clouds'
regurgitative rain, I can remember
all there was to know about that morning –
how the first light cracked across the flung-back
shutters of our windows, remaking all the shadows
of our crumpled skin-white bed. Sex

had nothing to do with it –
only the way I took your body as my body
in my hands – not knowing what to do with it,
myself, as each shy stroke began to form a canvas
stretching its colours to the livid natures of the night.
At least, that was the way I wanted to remember it,
and called it being in love. And would I be lying
if I added, too, just how intrigued I was,
quietly concerned? Like the first time
as a child, cutting my finger, smelling the blood.

Following

Your silence rebukes me like a seraph's smile.
All Winter I have dreamed of you and her –
The fleshy double bed – wanting

To prise her from you with my tongue, to lick
The years' interiors, smooth
As the hennaed intimacy

Of a peach stone to a peach: to
Smash them irretrievably –
Those unimaginable symmetries –

The lost curve of a perfect shell
That no one ever managed to depict.
I say these words over to myself

Like spells, wanting to know the meaning
Of them wholly and exactly: *husband and wife* –
Changing their emphasis, pronunciation,

Their relation each to each. Outside it snows:
The shattering first fall, and our walls bloom
Like crocuses unfurling in the dark. *Her name was*

Helen. It could only last ten years. That was
Your sad, half-hearted joke. Now
There is nothing to be said. In the half-light
Your daughter reads, looks up from time to time.

She has her mother's soft, uncanny ways.
And her blue eyes that laugh, and mesmerize me.
I watch them as they hatch like silk.

I know exactly the sort of woman I'd like to fall in love with

If I were a man.

And she would not be me, but
Older and graver and sadder.
And her eyes would be kinder;
And her breasts would be fuller;
The subtle movements
Of her plum-coloured skirts
Would be the spillings of a childhood summer.

She would speak six languages, none of them my own.

And I? I would not be a demanding lover.
My long fingers, with her permission
Would unravel her plaited hair;
And I'd ask her to dance for me, occasionally,
Half-dressed on the moon-pitted stairs.

BIOGRAPHICAL NOTES

WAYNE BURROWS was born in Derby in 1965. He moved to Aberaeron in 1978 and was educated there and at South East Derbyshire College. He has worked in a variety of fields, including antique restoration, with his own 'Root and Branch' theatre company partnership and as a designer and illustrator at Midland Railway Centre. He is presently a freelance writer/illustrator, working as a theatre/visual arts editor for the magazine *Overall There Is a Smell of Fried Onions* and as an arts contributor for *City Life* magazine. His poetry has appeared in *Seren Poets One: The Bloodstream* (1989) and *Poetry Wales: 25 Years* (1990). He is currently studying for an MA at Sheffield Hollom University and working on a book-length sequence, *Acid*, short stories, cartoon strips and a full-length illustrated book. He lives in Nottingham.

JACKIE KAY was born in Scotland in 1961. Her first collection, *The Adoption Papers*, was published by Bloodaxe Books in 1991. It received a Scottish Arts Council Book Award, a Saltire First Book of the Year Award and a Forward Prize in 1992 and was also shortlisted for the *Mail on Sunday*/John Llewellyn Rhys Prize. Her book of poetry for children, *Two's Company*, (Blackie, 1992), won the Signal Poetry Award in 1993. *Other Lovers* was published by Bloodaxe Books in 1993. She has written widely for stage and television. She lives in London.

RODDY LUMSDEN was born in St Andrews in 1966. He studied at Madras College, Edinburgh University and the School of Scottish Studies. His work has appeared in *Poetry Introduction 8* (Faber and Faber, 1993) and *Dream State: The New Scottish Poets* (Polygon, 1993). He lives in Edinburgh.

GLYN MAXWELL was born in 1962 in Welwyn Garden City, the second son of an industrial chemist and an actress. After English at Oxford he worked in Geneva. In 1987 he won a major scholarship in poetry and playwriting at Boston University, where he studied under Derek Walcott. *Tale of the Mayor's Son*

(Bloodaxe Books, 1990) was a Poetry Book Society Choice and was shortlisted for the *Mail on Sunday*/John Llewellyn Rhys Prize and the *Sunday Times* Young Writer's Award. *Out of the Rain* (Bloodaxe Books, 1992) was shortlisted for the 1992 Whitbread Poetry Prize and the 1993 Somerset Maugham Award. *Gnyss the Magnificent: Three Verse Plays* was published by Chatto and Windus in 1993.

STEPHEN SMITH was born in Worcestershire in 1964. He moved to Wales in 1978 and graduated from University College Wales, Aberystwyth in 1987. After two years' doctoral research he worked as a hospital cleaner and life model and then taught in Japan. *The Fabulous Relatives* was published by Bloodaxe in 1993. He teaches Creative Writing at Sutton College of Liberal Arts and is writing his second collection. He lives in Croydon.

JILL DAWSON was born in 1962 in Durham and grew up in West Yorkshire. She has twice worked as a writer-in-residence: in Doncaster and in Fareham, Hampshire. She is the editor of two books for teenagers, *School Tales* (The Women's Press, 1989) and *How Do I Look?* (Virago Upstarts, 1991) and two for adults, *The Virago Book of Wicked Verse* (Virago, 1992) and *The Virago Book of Love Letters* (Virago, 1994). Her poetry has appeared in numerous newspapers and magazines and in *Virago New Poets* (Virago, 1993), *The Virago Book of Birth Poetry* (Virago, 1993) and a Slow Dancer Press pamphlet, *White Fish with Painted Nails* (1993). Her short stories are included in *Erotica* (ed. Margaret Reynolds, Pandora Press, 1991) and *A Girl's Best Friend* (ed. Christina Dunhill, The Woman's Press, 1989). She lives in Hackney, London, with her young son.

HUGH DUNKERLEY began writing regularly in the late eighties and since then has been juggling writing with teaching. His work has appeared in a number of magazines and anthologies including *Orbis, Stand* and *Giant Steps*. In 1987/88 he spent a year at Lancaster University studying for an MA in Creative Writing. He also writes for children. He teaches Creative Writing at the West Sussex Institute of Higher Education and lives in Chichester.

CHRISTOPHER GREENHALGH was born in Manchester in 1963 and educated at the Universities of Hull and East Anglia. After living and working abroad for five years he returned to England in 1990 to undertake a PhD on the poetry of Frank O'Hara, which he finished in 1993. His first collection, *Stealing the Mona Lisa*, is published in 1994. He is married and lives in Kent.

MARITA MADDAH was born in Hertfordshire in 1963. The daughter of missionaries, she spent her early childhood in Ethiopia, returning to England in 1969. She studied English in Essex, where she was influenced by American Poetry. She trained in TEFL and taught briefly in Finland and then trained as an RGN at Charing Cross Hospital. Her work has appeared in *Poetry Review, Orbis*, the *Rialto* and the *Observer*. She is now working on her first collection and bringing up her three-year-old daughter. She lives in Essex.

STUART PATERSON was born in Truro in 1966. He has been writing poetry with any seriousness since 1989 and his work has appeared in *Dream State: The New Scottish Poets* (Polygon, 1993) and various reviews in Britain and abroad, including *Envoi, Chapman* and *Lines Review*. He received a Scottish Arts Council Writers' Bursary in 1993.

STUART PICKFORD was born in Canterbury and educated at the University of Lancaster and St Martin's College, Lancaster. His work has appeared in *Risk Behaviour* and *Spoils* (Smith/Doorstop Books) and various other journals. He is an English teacher at St Aidan's Comprehensive School, Harrogate.

SEAN BOUSTEAD was born in 1969 and brought up in Salford. He read Literature at Essex University. He has worked as a store assistant, postman, painter and decorator, builder's assistant, librarian, kitchen assistant and pizza chef. His work has appeared in *Agenda, Envoi* and *Guardian of the State* (*Poetry Now* anthology). He is currently working on translations of Italian, Spanish, French and Portuguese poets and a long verse narrative. He lives in Swinton, Greater Manchester.

ELEANOR BROWN was born in 1969, the third of seven children, and was brought up on the outskirts of Glasgow. She read English Literature at York University and, having been cast out into a deep recession, has obstinately refused to compromise with materialism by teaching English as a foreign language. She has kept her ideals, principles and self-sufficiency intact by working fifty-hour weeks as a waitress and writing in her spare time. She currently lives in France and is working on her first volume of poetry, *Maiden Speech*.

TRACEY HERD was born in East Kilbride in 1968. She graduated from Dundee University with an MA in English and American Studies in 1991. Her work has appeared in *Gallimaufry* (Dundee University arts magazine), *Aquarius, New Women Poets* (ed. Carol Rumens, Bloodaxe Books, 1990), *Duende: A Dundee Anthology* (ed. W. N. Herbert and Richard Price) and, to be published, *Writing Women*. She lives in Dundee and works in a bookshop.

JOEL LANE was born in Exeter in 1963 and was brought up in Birmingham. He read History and Philosophy of Science at Trinity College, Cambridge. His work has appeared in *Ambit, Foolscap, Oxford Poetry* and *Private Cities*, a three-poet anthology (Stride Publications, 1993). He lives in Birmingham and works in educational publishing and as a freelance writer.

ANGELA McSEVENEY was born in 1964 and brought up in Scotland, the youngest of five daughters. She graduated from Edinburgh University in 1986 and worked mainly as a library assistant until 1990, when she received a Scottish Arts Council Writers' Bursary. She has since worked as a cleaner, a telephone interviewer and a ticket seller at an historic house. Her work has appeared in *Coming Out With It* (Polygon, 1993) and the *New Edinburgh Review* (1986). She lives in Edinburgh.

DERYN REES-JONES was born in Liverpool in 1968. She read English at University College of North Wales, Bangor and is currently completing a doctoral thesis at Birkbeck College, London on the poetry of Sylvia Plath, Carol Ann Duffy, Medbh McGuckian and Selima Hill. Her first collection, *The Memory Tray*, will be published by Seren in 1994. She lives in London.

ACKNOWLEDGEMENTS

WAYNE BURROWS
Poetry Wales, Anglo-Welsh Review, Planet, Spectrum, Seren Poets One: The Bloodstream (ed. Ceri Meyrick), Seren, *Poetry Wales: 25 years* (ed. Cary Archard), Seren.

JACKIE KAY
The Adoption Papers, Bloodaxe Books, 1991; *That Distance Apart*, Bernard Stone, 1991.

RODDY LUMSDEN
'The Bedroom at Arles' and 'Vanishing' – *Poetry Introduction 8*, Faber and Faber, 1993.

GLYN MAXWELL
'La Brea' and 'Errand Boy' – *Times Literary Supplement*; 'Love Made Yeah' – *The New Poetry*, Bloodaxe Books; 'Eyes and Bones on Song' – *Poetry Review*; 'Out of the Rain XXXVII' – *Verse*; 'La Brea', 'Errand Boy' and 'Out of the Rain XXXVII' – *Out of the Rain*, Bloodaxe Books, 1992.

STEPHEN SMITH
'Letters to Myself, I–IV' and 'The Ringers' – *The Fabulous Relatives*, Bloodaxe Books, 1993; 'Letters to Myself, IV' – *The Forward Book of Poetry*, Sinclair-Stevenson, 1993; 'Ulster Holiday' – *The Fabulous Relatives* and *The Honest Ulsterman*.

JILL DAWSON
'The Mechanic' – *Ambit*; 'Arrina' – *Women Now*; 'For My Sister' – *Writing Women*; 'Paean' – *The Virago Book of Wicked Verse*.

HUGH DUNKERLEY
'Swift Mockery' and 'Geese' – *Giant Steps* (ed. Graham Mort), 1989.

CHRISTOPHER GREENHALGH
'Coffee-Break' – *Verse*; 'Islands' – *Bête-Noire*; 'The Night I Met

Marilyn' – *Bête-Noire, Poetry With an Edge*, Bloodaxe Books, 1993 and BBC Radio 4's *Time for Verse*.

MARITA MADDAH
'The Sunflowers' and 'Blood for Rain' – *Orbis*; 'Song for Ali Tiko' (revised version) – *The Rialto*.

STUART PATERSON
'Sandend 1989' and 'Gigha' – *Northlight*, issue 4, 1992; 'Garrier at Midnight' – *Pennine Platform*, issue 2, 1992; 'Silversmith' – *Spectrum*, issue 2, 1991.

STUART PICKFORD
'Over a Foreign Land' – *Outposts* and *Spoils*, Smith/Doorstop Books; 'mother finally...' – commended in National Poetry Competition 1984 and appeared in their prize-winning anthology and *Prospice* and *Risk Behaviour*, Smith/Doorstop Books; 'Cutting Dad's Nails' – *Tears in the Fence*; 'Port le Grand' – *The Pen*; 'Surrealism' – *Inkshed*.

TRACEY HERD
'A Searching Pace' – *Duende: A Dundee Anthology* (ed. W. N. Herbert and Richard Price).

JOEL LANE
'Engaged' – *Foolscap*; 'Energy and Silence' – *Private Cities*, Stride Publications; 'Messages' – *Ambit* and *Private Cities*; 'Gravel Tides' – *Oxford Poetry*.

DERYN REES-JONES
'Following' – runner-up in the Yorkshire Open Poetry Competition; 'The Chair' is dedicated to S.H.